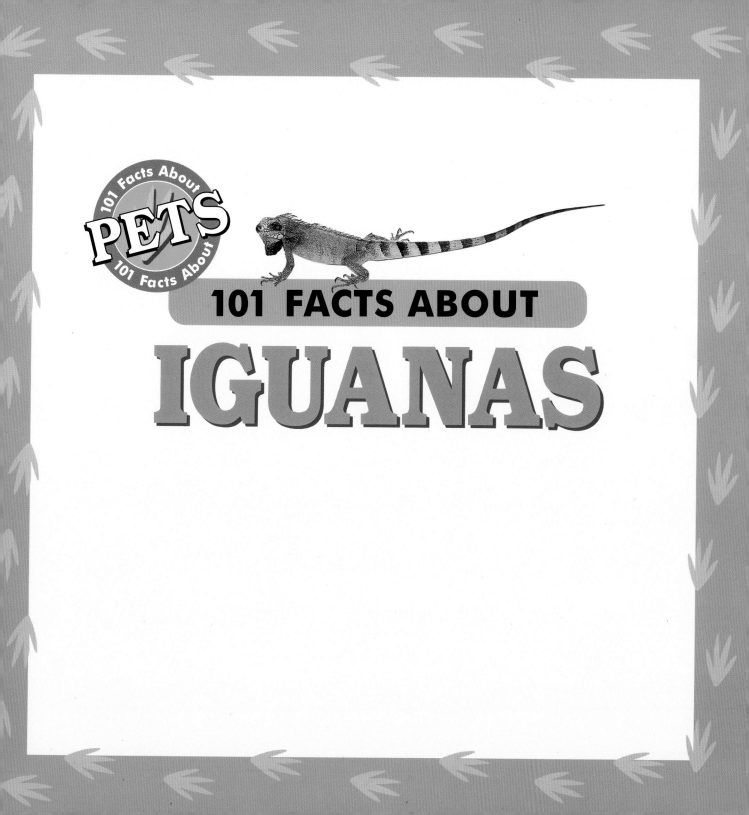

# 101 FACTS ABOUT

# IGUANAS

Published by Ringpress Books Limited,
PO Box 8, Lydney, Gloucestershire,
GL15 4YN, United Kingdom.

Design: Sara Howell

First Published 2001
© 2001 RINGPRESS BOOKS LIMITED

**ISBN 1 86054 158 5**

Printed in Hong Kong through Printworks Int. Ltd.

0 9 8 7 6 5 4 3 2 1

101 Facts About PETS
101 Facts About

# 101 FACTS ABOUT
# IGUANAS

**Sarah Williams**

Ringpress Books

**2** Reptiles are a large group of **ectothermic** (cold-blooded) creatures. This means they cannot make their own body heat, and need a heat source to be able to move.

**1** All iguanas are lizards. Lizards have been around for more than 260 million years. They are part of a bigger family, known as reptiles, which includes snakes, turtles, and tortoises.

**3** There are 44 **species** (kinds) of iguana, but most people keep the common or green iguana. The scientific name for this species is *Iguana iguana*.

**4** The name 'iguana' comes from 'iwana'. This was the name used by native American Caribbean Indians to describe all lizards. Spanish explorers translated *iwana* into iguana, and the name has stuck.

**5** All iguanas are **endangered** species. This means that there are so few of them that they may die out altogether. To stop this happening, iguanas are protected by laws.

**6** Iguanas hatch from eggs. Each clutch (group of eggs) may contain up to 60 eggs, but the average is 20 to 24. These eggs are laid deep underground.

**7** A baby iguana is about seven inches (18 centimetres) long.

**8** Adult iguanas can reach seven feet (two metres) in length, and can weigh up to 25-30 pounds (11-13.5 kilos).

**9** Most iguanas share the same basic features and habits. Some live in trees, and others also live on the ground.

**10** To help them balance in the trees most iguanas have a long tail. This tail can grow up to two or three times the length of the iguana's body.

**11** An iguana's toes and claws also help him to hold on to tree branches. The iguana's toes are called **digits**. The front feet have five digits, just like people, but the back feet only have four digits.

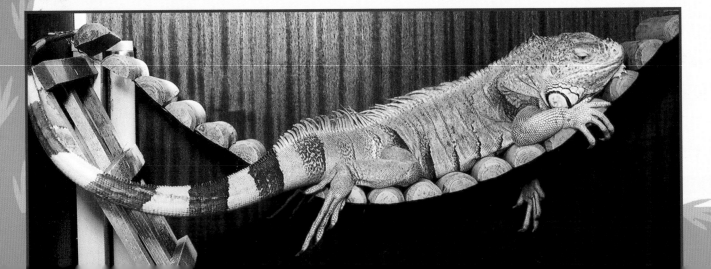

**14** The green iguana isn't always green! Some from Brazil can appear quite blue. Others, such as Mexican iguanas, are very orange.

**12** As well as the two eyes in its face, an iguana has an eye on the top of its head. It is called the **parietal eye**, and has nothing to do with seeing. Iguanas use it to tell the season.

**15** Whatever colour an iguana is at birth, the brightness of its skin will fade as it gets older.

**13** There are many different types of iguana, but the most common is the green iguana (also called the tree iguana).

7

**17** The chuckwalla iguana is very similar to the green iguana but, it is much fatter. In the wild it lives in the south-western American deserts.

**16** The green iguana (above) can be found in the wild in central and southern America, northern Mexico, Paraguay, the Antilles islands, and, more recently, in parts of the United States (such as Florida).

**18** The Desert iguana does not live in trees. It lives in the deserts of Mexico. It looks like the green iguana but is smaller.

**19** Rhinoceros iguanas (left) and Rock iguanas are some of the biggest iguanas around. The are very expensive to buy.

**20** The Spiny-tailed iguana is also known as the Black iguana. It comes from Mexico, Panama and the Colombian islands.

**21** Spiny tails are formed from scales which stand upright rather than flat on the iguana's skin. Male iguanas use these spiny tails as a very frightening weapon.

**22** Other iguanas can use their tails as a way to defend themselves. The iguana is an unusual animal because its tail is *meant* to break in certain places.

**23** If it is caught by a predator (an animal which hunts other animals for food), or a trap, the iguana will deliberately break its tail – by shaking itself violently. The skin breaks with the bone, and the iguana is set free.

**24** A pet iguana still behaves very much as it would in the wild. Unlike cats and dogs, an iguana will never be a true house-pet, and you should remember this before deciding to buy one.

**25** Before you choose and buy an iguana, you will need to have a home ready for it when you bring it home.

**26** You can keep an iguana in a cage or an aquarium. Cages have better **ventilation**, making it easier for the iguana to breathe, and are easier to move and clean.

**27** A four-foot iguana (1.25 metres) needs a minimum cage size of six feet (1.8 metres) in length, 30 inches (76 centimetres) in breadth, and six feet (1.8 metres) in height.

**28** The bottom of your iguana's enclosure should be lined with a suitable material, known as **substrate**

**31** The iguana's cage should be placed in a safe, quiet spot, away from other pets. These could frighten the iguana.

**29** Newspapers, bark chips, gravel, or specially-made carpets are all good substrates.

**30** Do not use cat litter, household carpet, wood shavings or sand. These get stuck in the iguana's stomach and can cause a blockage. They also hold bacteria (germs) from the iguana's droppings, which can cause a chest infection.

**33** If you were to stay out in the sun for too long, you would get sunburned. This is because sunlight is made up of **ultraviolet** (UV) rays, which can burn things. Iguanas *need* these rays to stay healthy and active.

**34** Your iguana will need 8 to 12 hours of sunlight a day. You can buy a special reptile lamp, called an ultraviolet light or a fluorescent (extremely bright) light. These give the iguana the UV rays that it needs.

**32** The cage should be placed where the iguana can absorb natural sunlight. However, make sure that the sunlight is not too strong – especially if you have an aquarium – or your iguana will suffer from heat-stroke.

**35** Nothing is as good as natural light. Take your iguana outside regularly. Some owners like to use a sunning cage. This is a smaller, lightweight cage, which can be easily carried outside.

**36** Some iguanas can become **hyperactive** if they have too much natural sunlight. This means that they have too much energy, and run around like mad!

**37** You must keep careful control over the temperature in your iguana's cage.

**38** The temperature in your iguana's cage should be between 85 and 100 degrees **Fahrenheit** or 29-38 degrees **Celsius**. Never allow it to fall below 70 degrees Fahrenheit (21 degrees Celsius).

**39** You can control the temperature by providing a heat lamp. Heat lamps should always be placed outside the cage. If they get too close, iguanas can suffer from nasty burns.

**40** Iguanas like an area to sunbathe. Hot rocks, or a heat lamp focused on a tree branch, can provide this.

**41** Hot rocks (or **sizzle stones**) look like normal rocks but give out hea

**42** Hot rocks should be checked daily. Some can get too hot and can burn the iguana.

**43** There should be an area in the cage where the iguana can cool of

14

and your iguana will get a chance to use his skills.

**46** Once you have prepared the cage, you can buy your iguana. A large pet store, or a breeder, will offer you a wide choice.

**44** Iguanas like to hide when they are asleep, or if they are afraid. You can make your iguana's cool spot into a good hiding place by adding lots of plants.

**47** Do your homework. Make sure that the store knows a lot about keeping and caring for iguanas.

**45** In the wild, many iguanas live in trees, so climbing comes naturally to them. Put a tree branch or shelf in the cage,

**48** It is best to buy one iguana only, because they are very territorial. This means that they fight if another iguana comes too close to them.

**49** Some people like female iguanas better than males. This is because females do not tend to fight as much as the males.

**50** Male iguanas are bigger than females. They usually have a wider head than the female, as well as having much larger **femoral pores**.

**51** The femoral pores are a single row of little, round holes on the inside of the iguana's back legs. On the male, the pores produce a waxy discharge, used for marking territory.

and the bones will stick out. The rest of the iguana should be thin, bright green, and very alert. If it seems lethargic (sleepy), do not buy it.

**52** The best age to buy a pet iguana is between three and five months. At this age the iguana is old enough to be strong and healthy, but young enough to cope well with change.

**54** Don't buy an iguana which isn't hungry. A healthy iguana has a good appetite.

**53** Make sure that you buy a healthy baby iguana. It should have a full, thick tail base. If it is unwell, the tail base will be very thin

**55** Other signs of illness to look out for are swelling along the jaw, and a runny nose.

**56** Try not to buy an older iguana. Some may have been returned to the pet store because of bad behaviour. Ask the pet store manager why the iguana has been put up for sale.

**57** Never buy a wild iguana which has been captured to sell. Wild iguanas are not tame, and may never get used to humans.

**58** An iguana with a good personality will keep its eyes open, lick you, move around and stretch out a lot.

**59** Once you have chosen your iguana, transport it home from the pet store in a secure travelling box – such as a cardboard box, which has a lid with holes in.

**62** The correct way to hold an iguana is to support the chest and tail. Never grab an iguana.

**60** Once you get home, your iguana should be left alone in its cage for a week. This will give it time to get used to its new home.

**61** Although they are naturally shy, iguanas are very affectionate once their trust has been earned. Regular handling will help you and your iguana get to know each other.

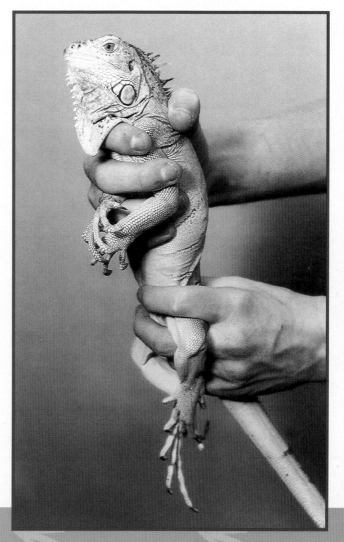

**63** Some iguanas become so tame that they will sit on their owner's shoulders, like a parrot. Others can wear a special lead (like a dog), and go for walks with their owners!

**64** If your iguana is very tame, it will climb on to your hand. You can make your iguana more tame by hand-feeding it.

**65** Iguanas are **folivores**. This means they are leaf-eating animals – they are completely vegetarian.

**66** All iguana food should be soft or shredded. Baby iguanas should have puréed (mashed or liquid) food.

**67** Iguanas need lots of **calcium** in their diet. Calcium is needed for bones to grow properly.

**68** The best way to ensure your iguana gets all its **vitamins** and **minerals** (things in food which are needed to be healthy) is to give it a special tablet or liquid, which you can buy from your pet shop.

**69** Just like people, iguanas like a varied diet. They can become bored if they are given the same food every day.

**70** Watch what your iguana eats. It will eat the things it likes, not what is good for it!

**71** Iguanas love lettuce. However, it is a bit like junk food for them, so keep it for special treats only.

**72** Commercial food mixes are not the best food for an iguana. Never give your iguana any more than 15 per cent of pre-mixed food as part of its overall diet.

**73** Apples, raspberries, avocado, dandelion greens and endive are all suitable foods for your iguana, but should not be given too regularly.

**74** Baby iguanas really like human baby food, and it is good for them too!

**75** Iguanas need lots of fresh water. Provide one bowl for drinking water, and a larger bowl for bathing. You should change the water every day.

**76** Iguanas should have a bath once a week. This keeps the iguana's skin clean and healthy.

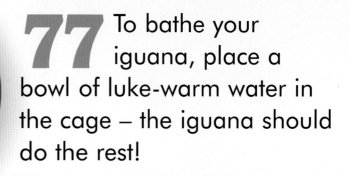

**77** To bathe your iguana, place a bowl of luke-warm water in the cage – the iguana should do the rest!

23

**78** The iguana should be able to bathe for up to three hours. Give it plenty of time to dry off afterwards.

**79** Like many reptiles, iguanas are good swimmers. Most iguanas love the water.

**80** Your iguana might like a large tub which can be used for the occasional swim. The water should always be warm, and the iguana should be able to climb out easily.

**81** Never use the family bath as an iguana swimming pool. Iguanas can shed a germ called **salmonella**. The next person to use the bath could catch it and become very ill.

**82** There are some chores which you will have to do every day or every week, to make sure that your iguana stays healthy.

**83** Once a week, you will have to clean your iguana's cage. The cage should be washed, and all the substrate should be replaced.

**84** Every day, spray the iguana's cage with water from a small spray bottle.

**85** Spraying prevents the iguana from becoming **dehydrated** (dried out), and helps shedding.

**86** Iguanas, like snakes, **shed** their skin. It comes off in pieces. From time to time, you may need to help your iguana remove a piece of skin.

**87** Although iguanas are very different pets to cats or dogs, they still need grooming. One of the most important things you can do for your iguana is to cut its nails.

**88** In the wild, an iguana's nails are its best weapon. They grow very long and sharp. When iguanas are kept as pets, the nails are not worn down so quickly, and, left too long, can easily injure the iguana – and you!

**89** Only snip off the ends of the nails. If you cut off too much, you will hurt the iguana and could even make it ill. Your vet will show you how to cut your iguana's nails.

**90** Make sure your vet has lots of experience of treating reptiles, and especially iguanas.

**93** All iguanas sneeze quite a lot. If yours sneezes more than normal, though, or if it is panting slightly, it may have a chest infection, and you should take it to the vet.

**91** Check the health of your iguana every day. Look to see if it has eaten all its food, and make sure it is bright and alert.

**94** Common problems with iguanas are burns, cuts and grazes, nose rubbing, mites, ticks, and broken nails. Your vet can help treat these.

**92** Signs of ill health are: a runny nose, swelling, colour changes, and cuts or grazes on the iguana's skin.

**95** More serious illnesses include broken legs, salmonella, metabolic bone disease, kidney disease, and breathing problems. Your vet will hopefully treat these too.

**96** One day, your iguana may look after you! A man in New York claims that, when he collapsed with a heart attack, his iguana saved his life – by knocking the phone off the hook and accidently calling the ambulance.

**97** Some iguana keepers who have been looking after iguanas for years, like to breed their pets. This can be very exciting, but it is best left to the experts.

**98** Breeding iguanas is not especially hard, but it takes up a lot of room! You will need lots of cages for the babies, and make sure the mum and dad have enough space to keep out of each other's way – otherwise they will fight.

**100** Males and females both have crests, but only the male can ruffle its scales to make his crest bigger and more eye-catching.

**101** If you look after your iguana carefully, you will be rewarded with a happy, friendly, and very unusual pet.

**99** When the male and female are mating (or fighting!) the male will show off its crest – a row of large pointy scales running down the length of the back.

# GLOSSARY

**Calcium:** a mineral needed to have strong, healthy bones.

**Celsius:** a scale (like centimetres on a ruler) to measure heat.

**Dehydrated:** dried out.

**Digits:** an iguana's toes.

**Ectothermic:** cold-blooded creatures which can only move around when they are warm.

**Endangered species:** animals that are so small in number, they may become extinct.

**Fahrenheit:** like Celsius, a scale to measure heat.

**Femoral pores:** small, round holes on the iguana's back legs.

**Folivores:** animals that eat only leafy foods.

**Hyperactive:** having too much energy.

**Mineral/Vitamins:** the part of your food which keeps your body healthy (see Calcium).

**Parietal eye:** the Iguana's third eye which is on top of its head.

**Salmonella:** a germ carried by some iguanas which can make people very ill.

**Shed:** where the iguana gets rid of its old, dead skin.

**Sizzle stone:** a heated rock which the iguana can lie on to get warm.

**Species:** a group or type of animal. For example, humans are one species, and iguanas are another.

**Substrates:** the materials used to line the bottom of a cage.

**Ultraviolet:** part of what makes up sunlight. UV can be harmful to people but is necessary for iguanas to be healthy.

**Ventilation:** the ability for air to move around.

# MORE BOOKS TO READ

**All About Your Iguana**
Chris Newman
(Ringpress Books)

**My Pet Iguana**
Amy Adams
(Shining Lights Press)

**Iguanas (Exotic Lizards series)**
W. P. Mara
(Capstone Press)

**Your Pet Iguana**
Elaine Landau
(Children's Press)

# WEBSITES

**Iguana Den**
www.iguanaden.com

**About Iguanas**
www.sonic.net/~melissk/aabout.html

**Iguana Awareness**
www.niad.org/

**Little Lucy's Page**
members.aol.com/mylittlelu

For additional websites, use a reliable search engine to find one or more of the following key words: **iguana, green iguana, iguana care, lizards, reptiles.**

# INDEX